Fruit Infused Water

26 REFRESHING *VITAMIN WATER RECIPES* TO
REHYDRATE, REJUVENATE AND SUPERCHARGE YOUR HEALTH

Disclaimer

Table of Contents

4

Introduction

Your body is sixty percent water. You're pumping with blood and full of life-sustaining organs—things that require proper hydration in order to function properly. Your lungs, for example, are ninety percent water, your brain is seventy percent water, and your blood, of course, is over eighty percent water.

But you're losing water all the time.

For example, you sweat out approximately two cups of water per day, depending on your size. You do this through every day activities. But you sweat out quite a bit more if you're active. When you exhale normally throughout the day, you lose more than a cup of water from your body. If your exercise level is higher than average, you tend to exhale much more during physical activity. Therefore, you lose extra water. And, of course, you use the bathroom and expel something like six cups of liquid per day. You're losing water all the time, and you need to keep your body hydrated with healthy, natural liquids constantly.

Drinking more water seems like the natural solution. It keeps you rejuvenated, fresh-faced, and healthy. It keeps your blood pumping heartily from your brain to your toe muscles. It allows your digestive system to function properly. It also retains your skin's flexibility and youth. And yet, our culture finds it incredibly difficult to consume enough water on a daily basis. We are a 'forever' dehydrated society. This is mostly due to the fact that there are several other, sugar-based options: things like soda pop, energy drinks, juices. However, many of these drinks we reach for when we're "thirsty" are filled with sugar. These sugary drinks actually make us thirstier; it requires quite a bit more water to digest the sugar contained in the drinks than the drinks administer.

The solution to our hydration problem, however, does not have to drop the flavor and vibrant color of the popular juice and soda drinks. Fruit infused water contains all the needed hydration of regular water with the added taste of your favorite fruits, teas, and herbs. This recipe book provides easy examples of these infused drinks—things you can prepare every day for continuous hydration. You can utilize things you have around your house: herbs from your garden and fruits of the season. Don't allow your oranges and apples to go to waste: simply toss them in a pitcher and allow the infusion magic to charge itself. The water infusion lifestyle is broad, inclusive. It simply asks you to do the very thing your body requires: drink water. Do it with style. Each infused drink brings a breath of fresh, natural color to your world. You'll feel like you're drinking a fresh treat: you'll both feel and see the results of adding more hydration to your diet, as well.

Furthermore, each fruit and herb extends the reach of its nutritive properties into your ordinary water—without so many of the calories. Therefore, if you love the taste of apple but can't handle the carbohydrates right now, your apple nutrients will leek—vitamin C included—into your water. You can remove the plant-based carbohydrate-rich apple and simply retain its water.

The rejuvenating infused water recipes in this book are divided into sections: Citrus-based, Tea-based, Herb-based, Winter-fruit based, and Summer-fruit based. Each category maintains a separate aspect of your health. Each category fuels a different aspect of your diet. Therefore, if you're currently operating under a reduced calorie diet or are simply finding yourself void of proper nutrients, infusing your water is an excellent way to assimilate back to health.

Chapter 1

DEHYDRATION AND YOUR BODY:
What You Need to Know

Your body's crazy for water. The H2O pulsing through your system is your bread and butter, the only thing keeping you here alive and well. You are, after all, approximately 60% water. Water is the literal fuel that allows your metabolic processes to embark swiftly and coolly throughout your body; it is the very thing allowing these metabolic processes to create energy from the food and drink you consume, thus allowing you to process energy correctly—and subsequently stay alive. The best part? In much of the world, water is free and ready to pulse your metabolism and create a cleaner, more preserved body system. And yet millions of people around the world suffer from dehydration and its rampant effects every day.

Understand the precise ways in which dehydration can destroy you: cell-by-cell. Understand the ways in which just a few changes—the additions of the fruit infused vitamin water included in this very book—can assist in reversing this unrest in your system.

Memory Impairment

Dehydration causes memory loss. When your brain does not have enough fluids, your cells cannot communicate properly. In order to create short-term memories, your neurons must fire in a very specific way in your hippocampus. Cell to cell communication relies heavily on the area in between the cells. Having proper hydration surrounding your brain cells allows proper flushing of these cells, as well. Your brain cells must expel the waste from their interior; they must take in new nutrition from the surrounding liquid. If the surrounding liquid is not substantial, your cell cannot expel waste. It cannot take in new nutrients. And therefore, it will have trouble properly communicating with its next-door neighbor cell. If it cannot communicate, it cannot create these neuron "pathways" that create memories. If you have a few foggy places in your memory from the past few days for an inexplicable reason, you may have been dehydrated. You cannot recreate these moments, and therefore your brain has no way to retrace the neuron pathways.

Digestion Inhibition and Increased Appetite

Oftentimes when you think you're hungry, you're actually thirsty. Therefore, you'll have another helping, another snack—for no reason. You'll intake extra calories which can lead to weight gain and bloating. Furthermore, staying hydrated is important for proper digestion. You must flush out the waste of any foods you've imbibed by drinking plenty of water. Hydration will allow your food to be properly filtrated in your kidney. Afterwards, your body can expel the waste from your food while accepting the nutrients, tacking the nutrients to your bloodstream, and sending them out to your important organs.

Reduced Ability to Maintain Temperature

Maintaining your hydration is incredibly important to retain your proper body temperature. When your interior muscles contract, they generate the heat the rest of your body requires. Therefore, your blood must deliver this heat to your exterior portions. In order for you blood to maintain this heat, it must continue to have appropriate blood pressure. Blood pressure relies heavily on your hydration. When you are dehydrated, your body must work continually harder to keep your blood pressure on par. When your blood pressure drops, your muscles retain your heat to your deep interior and do not deliver the heat to your exterior. Therefore, your skin will be cool and clammy.

Dehydration Hinders Kidney Functionality

Dire dehydration can ultimately lead to kidney failure. The kidneys are responsible for pumping nutrient-rich blood throughout your body to all of your organs. Therefore, your kidneys are ultimately responsible for a great portion of your body: from your brain to your digestive system to your leg muscles. If these organs do not receive the proper hydration, they begin to shut down.

Your kidney filters the blood in your body and dispels waste from your body in your urine. However, when your body becomes dehydrates, your kidneys retain water. Therefore, the water they retain contains much of this unnecessary waste. Unnecessary waste blocks your kidneys from proper filtration. Therefore, the blood in your body is not as impactful for your organs.

Rampant Stress: A Pathway to Additional Dehydration

An unfortunate truth of life is this: stress causes dehydration and dehydration causes stress. It seems like there's no way around it; it's a vicious cycle taking its toll on your every day activities. Dehydration is making your already stress-filled existence something out of control and constant.

The reason for this dehydration and stress relation is found in your brain. When your body finds itself lacking a certain amount of hydration, cortisol kicks in. Cortisol is a stress hormone that's activated during the fight or flight response; it's the hormone our ancestors needed in order to maintain their survival. However, present-day humans have spikes in cortisol levels all the time; unfortunately, it is increasingly more difficult to reduce the levels of cortisol in the blood. Increased cortisol levels cause a wealth of disruptions in your body. Cortisol attacks your brain functions, impairing your memory and your ability to maintain your weight.

When you are stressed from life events, your body begins to work in a sort of overdrive. Your heart beats heavy, your blood starts pumping more quickly around your body. And all this activity requires more and more water as you flush your hydration out quickly via body processes. However, after this preliminary stress causes you to flush your hydration from your body, your cortisol stress hormone can actually skyrocket. Studies have proven that decreasing your body's fluids by just half a liter can help cortisol with its peppy field day. Therefore, stress leads to more cortisol. And cortisol leads to more stress. This continued stress adds additional elements, as well, beyond the obvious ones: prepare for fatigue, headaches, and a bit of nausea.

Chapter 2

DAILY WATER REQUIREMENTS

Numbers are spouted wildly when considering the amount of water we need in order to properly function on a cellular level. However, no true number works across the board. The amount of water you need is based on your size, the amount of stress you have, your basic exercise and activity level, and the climate in which you live.

Therefore, if you exercise very little and live in a cold environment, you do not expel as much water as someone who exercises quite a bit and lives in a hot climate. The more water you expel on a daily basis, the more water you need to drink to maintain a happy balance.

Furthermore, a general rule to think about with regards to water intake is based on your size. Drink a half an ounce of water or more per pound of your body weight. Therefore, if you weigh 160 pounds, you must drink at least eighty ounces of water per day. If you exercise or are under great duress, you should spike that number as close to 160 as you can. As aforementioned, this number of ounces has many, many factors.

Luckily, approximately twenty percent of our fluid intake can be found in the foods we eat. If your diet is rich in fruits and vegetables, you are helping your body to greater hydration all the time. For example, cucumbers, celery, and watermelon are all nearly 100% water; nutrient-rich, vibrant broccoli rolls in at 89% water, as well.

The other 80% of our hydration must come in the form of water, tea, and various other beverages: tiny amounts of caffeinated or caloric beverages, perhaps. Remember to drink sugary drinks, alcohol, and caffeinated drinks sparingly. All of these beverages tend to promote dehydration and loss of fluids.

Chapter 3

WATER DEFICIENT WARNING SIGNS

When your body doesn't receive enough hydration, it lets you know in increasingly dire ways. When you become initially dehydrated, you will, of course, become thirsty. This is the first warning sign: this discomfort. But humans have learned to feed this discomfort with sugary drinks. Therefore, your body will move on to the next steps. Your mouth will become dry; your eyes will stop making tears. If you feel your contacts begin to dry out, for example, you may be dehydrated.

Your body will begin to retain water, and therefore, any urine you expel will be incredibly concentrated and yellow. You may stop sweating. Therefore, your body's temperature will have difficulty maintaining itself.

Eventually, dehydration will lead to muscle cramps, nausea, and heart palpitations. You will feel dizzy and confused. This is because your body is trying to maintain your original cardiac output; it is trying to continue to pump the same amount of blood from the heart to the rest of your body without the same amount of fluids. However, your body attempts to do this by constricting your blood vessels in order to keep your blood pressure up. Your blood shrinks away from your skin in order to retreat to your organs.

It is especially important to monitor the hydration levels of children and the elderly. Dehydration can affect them much more drastically; however, they are often less aware of their body and their body's hydration levels. Therefore, if you notice a member of your family beginning to look confused, feel his skin and check his pulse. If his pulse is high and his skin is clammy, be sure to fuel him with water.

Luckily, there are several fruit, herb, and tea infused vitamin water techniques that allow staying hydrated to be an easy, fun adventure in the kitchen. Keep a few fruits and herbs on hand at all times in case you begin to experience the symptoms above. Remember that staying hydrated is a lifelong goal. It will keep you youthful and fresh every day of your life.

Chapter 4

FRUIT, HERB, AND TEA INFUSED VITAMIN WATER RECIPES

Citrus-Based Recipes

Citrus fruits are delicious and refreshing. But beyond that, they have incredible nutritive properties to boost your health. They contain something called flavonoids that are responsible for a number of wonderful things. For example, flavonoids prevent the growth and spread of cancer cells. They also neutralize any free radicals or waste created and expelled from your cells. Free radicals can do a great deal of damage; they can work to kill skin cells, for example, and cause early wrinkles to form.

Furthermore, vitamin C in citrus fruits actually works to eliminate the fight or flight hormone, cortisol. Thus, if you intake enough vitamin C, you'll work to reduce your stress: the very stress that causes increased dehydration.

The Vitamin-C stress-reducing aspects of this infused water are divine; however, this Citrus-Based recipe includes brain-healthy blueberries as well—nature's remedy for memory saving and creation.

Note: This recipe calls for blueberries; they can be found for a much cheaper price in the frozen section. However, if you utilize frozen blueberries and not fresh blueberries, it's important to allow the water to infuse at room temperature for several hours prior to sending it off to the refrigerator.

Note: Be wary of lemon. A little bit is perfect; too much is a blast of sour.

Recipe for 32 oz. Container

Ingredients:
2 oranges slices
1 lemon slice
10 blueberries

Directions:
Add the ingredients to filtered water and allow them to infuse either at room temperature (for frozen blueberries) or in the fridge (for fresh blueberries) for four to eight hours. Maximum

flavor occurs after twenty-four hours. Pour your citrus-based vitamin water over ice and enjoy!

Lemon-Lime Zest Vitamin Water

Note: Utilizing the rind of the lemon or lime creates an automatic bitterness. If you are planning to drink your infused water for several days, do not infuse your lemon and lime with the rind on as the bitterness will escalate over time.

Recipe for 32 oz. Jar

Ingredients:
2 lemon slices
2 lime slices

Directions:
Add your lemon and lime slices to your filtered jar water—with or without the rind based on your appropriate usage. Infuse the water for six hours in the refrigerator. Serve chilled, and enjoy!

Citrus Fruit Family Infused Water

Recipe for 32 oz. Jar

Ingredients:
½ orange, sliced
¼ grapefruit, sliced
½ lemon, sliced
½ lime, sliced

Directions:
Add the sliced pieces of fruit to a jar and fill the jar with mineral water. Allow the water to infuse in the refrigerator for six to eight hours. The result is a vitamin-rich, vibrant hydration mixture!

Vanilla Orange Sunny Day Infused Water

Recipe for 2-Quart Pitcher

Ingredients:
1 orange, sliced
½ tsp. vanilla

Directions:
Slice the orange into thin strips. The more surface area you allow, the more orange and delicious your water will be. Plop the orange slices and the vanilla into your 2-quart pitcher. Next, fill the pitcher with mineral water. Allow the pitcher to sit in the refrigerator for just an hour prior to serving. Enjoy your delicious twist of orange infused water with a delightful hint of vanilla.

Note: This recipe calls for one lemon and water. That's it. Simple, right? But there's nothing entirely more delicious than this simplicity. Furthermore, the simple lemon water allows for proper digestion.

Recipe for 32 Oz. Jar

Ingredients:
1 lemon, sliced

Directions:
Slice the lemon into five or six pieces. Pop them into your 32-ounce jar and add water. Allow the water to infuse in the refrigerator for four hours prior to serving. Enjoy your refreshing treat. This simple recipe is a hit at any summer party.

Tea-Based Recipes

Tea has long been proclaimed to rev a lulling metabolism. This is because tea contains catechins: an antioxidant that actually decreases hunger. Furthermore, several teas have been linked to staving off cancer. Stay hydrated, lose a bit of weight, and ward off cancer cells with the following delicious infused water treats!

Note: The Heavenly Hibiscus Vitamin Water lends a vibrant, beautiful color great for outdoor parties or events.

Recipe for 32 oz. Jar

Ingredients:
2 pieces of watermelon—approximately 1 inch by 4 inch in size
1 tsp. dried hibiscus

Directions:
Add your watermelon pieces and your dried hibiscus to your filtered jar water. Infuse the tea in the refrigerator for four hours. Afterwards, be sure to strain the tea prior to serving. Enjoy your delightful, healthy treat!

Note: Black Tea contains a bit of caffeine, ready to blast you through your day. However, it contains far less caffeine amounts than the typical coffee. It's important to create this black tea infused water with room temperature settings. Chilled tea doesn't allow for any infusion.

Recipe for 32 oz. Jar

Ingredients:
3 mandarin oranges, sliced
4 basil leaves, torn into pieces
1 black tea bag

Directions:
Add your sliced mandarin oranges, basil leaves, and black tea bag to your 32 oz. jar water. Infuse the ingredients at room temperature for three hours. Serve over ice, and enjoy.

Green Tea Mint Infused Water

Recipe for 6 oz. Jar

Ingredients:
1 green tea bag
1 sprig mint
2 slices lime

Directions:
Add your green tea packet, your slightly crushed mint sprig, and your two thinly sliced pieces of lime to your 6 oz. jar. Allow the mixture to infuse in your refrigerator for two hours. Prior to enjoying, remove your green tea packet and enjoy your delicious mixture of the cool, earthy tones of the green tea and the bright, fat-burning quality of the lime.

Strawberry-Chamomile Tea Infused Water

Recipe for 32 oz. Jar

Ingredients:
1 bag chamomile tea
1 strawberry, sliced
½ orange, sliced into two quarters

Directions:
Slice your strawberries to provide the greatest surface area of the interior of the fruit. Toss your strawberries, your orange slices, and your tea bag into a 32 oz. jar and add mineral water. Allow the water to infuse in the refrigerator for two to four hours prior to serving. Enjoy!

Raspberry Black Tea Infused Water

Recipe for 32 oz. Jar

Ingredients:
7 raspberries
1 black tea bag

Directions:
Toss your raspberries into a 32 oz. jar and muddle them a bit so that they release those mighty juices to your infused water. Add your tea bag as well. Pour water into the jar. Infuse the tea-based water at room temperature for maximum flavor. Remember that your normal tea will only infiltrate your water when it's hot; therefore, it will not activate in cold water. After four hours in room temperature, strain the raspberry tea. You may now keep the infused water in the refrigerator until you are ready to serve! Enjoy.

Herbal-Based Recipes

Herb-Based vitamin water brings some pep back to your skin. It rejuvenates the areas between your skin cells more quickly, allowing you to eliminate wrinkles and add an extra shine, an extra bit of youth to your exterior. Furthermore, herbs contain incredible antioxidants, as well, that curb inflammation throughout your body. With this reduced inflammation, you also reduce your chances of heart disease and cancer.

Recipe for 32 oz. Jar

Ingredients:
3 basil leaves, torn
1 sprig rosemary
2 sprigs dill
1 sprig lemon thyme

Directions:
Remember to tear your leaves prior to adding them to your jar water. Tearing them allows the taste to better assimilate into your drink. Infuse the herbs for six to eight hours in the refrigerator. Remember: the greater amount of time, the more your herbs will take flight. After the infusing process, strain out your leaves and enjoy chilled.

Rosemary and Cucumber Fresh Vitamin Water

Recipe for 2-Quart Pitcher

Ingredients:
6 cups chilled spring water
12 thin slices of cucumber
4 slices lemon
4 sprigs crushed mint
2 sprigs crushed rosemary

Directions:
Slice your cucumber and lemon and slightly crush your mint and rosemary. Pour the six cups chilled water into your pitcher, and then add your slices of cucumber, lemon, mint, and rosemary. Cover the pitcher and allow the water to infuse for up to eight hours. Serve chilled.

Recipe for 2-Quart Pitcher

Ingredients:
3 stems rosemary
6 thyme stems
12 sage leaves
Handful mint
Handful basil
2-inch piece ginger, sliced

Directions:
Begin by boiling four cups of mineral water. Add your herbs to a large, heat-proof container. After the water has boiled, pour it over the herbs. Allow the herbs to infuse with the boiling water until it cools. Next, add an additional four cups of mineral water—not boiled—to the pot. Transfer the entire pot of water to a large pitcher and allow the water to chill for two hours in the refrigerator.
Note: For a bit of sweetness, try adding a few berries to the tea upon serving.

Hint of Vanilla Lemongrass Infused Water

Recipe for Half Gallon

Ingredients:
1 stalk lemongrass, chopped and crushed
¼ cup peppermint, chopped
½ vanilla bean, sliced lengthwise

Directions:
Place the chopped lemongrass, peppermint, and vanilla bean into a half-gallon pitcher. Fill the pitcher with cold mineral water. Allow the pitcher to infuse for approximately eight hours. Next, strain the contents of the pitcher. Place the strained water back into the pitcher and enjoy! The infused water lasts for three days in the refrigerator.

Recipe for Half Gallon

Ingredients:
¾ cup fresh or frozen blackberries
¼ cup dried pink rose petals
½ vanilla bean, sliced lengthwise

Directions:
Place the blackberries—frozen or fresh—into a half-gallon pitcher along with the dried rose petals and the vanilla bean. Add mineral water to the pitcher and place it in the refrigerator. Allow the water to infuse for eight hours. Afterwards, strain the contents of the pitcher and return the clean water to the pitcher. Enjoy your beautiful, rose-tinted infused water!

Note: This is an easy, tasty, and instant infused water recipe. Utilize leftover fennel you have lying around for this fresh twist on infused water with a bit of sweetness.

Recipe for 32 oz. Jar

Ingredients:
Fennel tops
Carbonated water (filled to the top of the jar)

Directions:
Place the fennel tops into the carbonated water. The instant aroma will be irresistible. Enjoy your exotic-looking fennel drink containing heart-healthy antioxidants!

Summer Fruit-Based Recipes

The summer brings a wealth of fruit options. Look to your watermelons, strawberries, blueberries, blackberries, and raspberries. Oftentimes, you can utilize fruits that might be a little under ripe or overripe—things you might not want to munch on anymore—for these infused water recipes. Enjoy the smattering of flavors.

Much like the winter fruits, the summer fruits add a wealth of vitamins and minerals to your diet. It's important to soak up the watery fruits in the summer months as you sweat more often and exhale more water. Your body will be craving water at all times.

Summer Breeze Mango Vitamin Water

Note: This recipe works great with a semi-firm mango; your tireless days of searching for the perfect, ripe mango are over.

Recipe for 32 oz. Jar

Ingredients:
8 small leaves fresh mint
½ mango—peeled and divided into six pieces

Directions:
Add the mint leaves and the mango pieces to the water. Allow them to infuse for three to four hours at room temperature. The warmth allows aggressive flavor to erupt from your mango. However, you can also infuse the water for twelve hours in your refrigerator. After enjoying your drink, try eating the mango, as well! They're soft and ready despite their original semi-ripe qualities.

Spicy Strawberry Vitamin Water

Recipe for 32 oz. Jar

Ingredients:
3 strawberries
¼ to ½ jalapeno pepper

Directions:
Slice the strawberries to reveal their maximum surface area. Be sure to remove the green stems. Slice your allotted jalapeno pepper. Utilize some plastic gloves to deseed your pepper. You don't want to touch the juices!

Add the sliced strawberries and jalapenos to cold water. Allow the ingredients to infuse for three to twelve hours in the refrigerator. Remember, your drink heats up the colder it gets!

Note: One half of the jalapeno pepper makes the water spicy. If you like spice, then opt for this and no more. One quarter of the jalapeno pepper creates a very limited spice. If this is what you're into—go for it! Furthermore, the longer you choose to infuse your water, the spicier it will become. Your sweet summer strawberries will work to alternate the spiciness, however.

Note: This recipe tastes precisely like cherry limeade without the added sugar and calories. Delicious!

Recipe for 32 oz. Jar

Ingredients:
2 slices lime
4 pitted cherries

Directions:
Place ice in your jar—filling to approximately the halfway mark. Next, toss in your pitted cherries and your lime slices. Stir and allow the jar to sit at room temperature for two hours prior to enjoying. Best of all, you can leave the cherries and limes in the drink as you sip away, allowing for quite a pretty treat.

Note: Blackberries contain limitless antioxidants.

Recipe for 6 oz. Jar

Ingredients:
1 cup fresh or frozen blackberries
2 mint sprigs
6 oz. mineral water

Directions:
Add your blackberries and your mint sprigs to your jar. Pour the mineral water over the fruit and mint, and stir for thirty seconds. If you do not want blackberry chunks in your drink, you may strain the liquid to remove them. The chunks do not hurt the drink, of course. It's simply personal preference. Allow the mixture to infuse for two hours in the refrigerator prior to serving. Enjoy!

Red Raspberry Infused Water

Recipe for 32 oz. Jar

Ingredients:
2 stems mint with leaves
7 fresh raspberries

Directions:
Plop your mint leaves and your fresh raspberries into your 32 oz. jar and add mineral water. Allow the water to infuse for four hours in the refrigerator. Afterwards, you have a choice. You can strain the drink or not. If you choose not to, stir it up a little bit—muddling the raspberries. This allows the drink to become an even more vibrant color; it also allows even more flavor to escape. The infused water is the perfect crown on a long day of berry-picking.

Winter Fruit-Based Recipes

If you find yourself dragging through the winter months, you might not be drinking enough water or filling up on enough fruit juices. The winter months have their own share of fruits to choose from: flock to mandarin oranges (often bought easily in bulk!), lemons, apples, kiwis, clementines—the list is extensive!

It's important during the winter months to maintain your vitamin C and fiber intake. The winter months can be both stressful and hard on your body—especially if you spend any time outside in the cold. Eat your vitamins and minerals in order to maintain your insides so you can keep going.

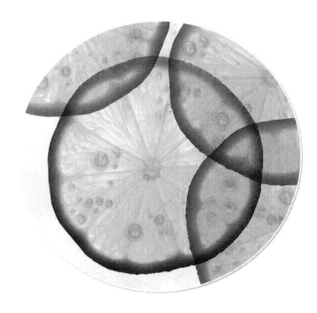

Winter Rejuvenation Vitamin Water

Note: This recipe utilizes winter fruits, sweet lemons and mandarin oranges.
Note: Leaving the lemon peel on the lemon while infusing makes the vitamin water naturally more bitter.

Recipe for 32 oz. Jar

Ingredients:
2 sweet lemons, ends removed, sliced
4 mandarin oranges, peeled and halved

Directions:
Add your sweet lemon slices and your mandarin orange halves to fresh, filtered water. Infuse at room temperature for two to six hours.

Recipe for 2-Quart Pitcher

Ingredients:
1 apple, thinly sliced
1 cinnamon stick

Directions:
Fill your 2-Quart pitcher with mineral water. Slice your apple slices as thinly as possible; the more surface area of your apples available, the better your taste will be. Add the apples and the cinnamon stick to the water. Allow the water to infuse in the refrigerator for two to three hours.

Note: Pomegranates and blueberries are fueled with many antioxidants, which are great for reducing inflamed cells in your brain. Feel immediately alert and well with the delicious aid of this winter fruit water.

Recipe for 2-Quart Pitcher

Ingredients:
1 pint blueberries
½ cup pomegranate seeds
2 quarters spring water

Directions:
You must begin by slicing a pomegranate in order to remove the seeds. Slice the pomegranate into quarters carefully. Next, add cold water to a large mixing bowl. Dunk the pomegranate quarters into the water in order to separate the seeds. After you've completed dunking the pomegranate, strain the cold water to remove the seeds.
Add the pomegranate seeds and the blueberries to a large, 2-Quart pitcher. Fill the pitcher with spring water. If you're utilizing frozen blueberries, allow the water to infuse at room temperature for three hours. If you're utilizing fresh blueberries, allow the water to infuse in the refrigerator for the same amount of time. Enjoy.

Orange-Cranberry Infused Water

Note: Cranberries are the classic winter fruit. You can usually buy fresh batches after Halloween.

Recipe for 32 oz. Jar

Ingredients:
2 oranges, sliced
3 cups frozen or fresh cranberries

Directions:
Slice the oranges without removing the peel. Add your orange slices and your cranberries to your jar, and add water. If you're utilizing frozen cranberries, allow the water to infuse at room temperature for two hours prior to serving. If you're utilizing fresh cranberries, allow the water to infuse in the refrigerator for two hours prior to serving.

Ginger-Pear Infused Water

Recipe for 2-Quart Pitcher

Ingredients:
5 pears
1 small lemon
6 cloves
2 cinnamon sticks

Directions:
Begin by coring and slicing the pear. You may leave the skin on. Next, squeeze one half of the lemon over the pear slices. This will keep the pear slices from turning brown.

Next, slice your other half of the lemon into neat, thin slices. Add the lemon slices, the pear slices, the cloves, and the cinnamon sticks to a 2-quart pitcher and add mineral water. Allow the water to infuse in the refrigerator for two to four hours.

After two hours, you may serve your delicious, infused drink! You can garnish with a cinnamon stick, if you like: this will add a little pep and a little spice to the already popping drink.

Conclusion

There's no life without water. In your personal, day-to-day life, there's no happiness without it. A life without proper hydration leads to stress, loss of memory, lack of comprehension—plain misery. But our world of sugary drinks and energy-quick caffeinated beverages has swayed us away from the natural remedy of just drinking a glass of hydrating water.

We have analyzed the ways in which dehydration is taking hold of your life and spinning it down the drain. We analyzed the ways in which you need water for a happier, skinnier, rejuvenated you.

But I also understand that, being human, you need some flavor—some spice in your life. What good is anything without a little fun? The recipes in this book lend you creative ways in which to create your own infused waters from the comfort of your home. You can utilize any sort of fruit you have lying around at home. With a little time and patience, you could be drinking beautiful, vibrant infused drinks and fueling yourself, little by little, with the magic of hydration.

Therefore, don't settle for a life of lack of health and sugary, corporate drinks. Don't settle for tasteless water, either. Find yourself your favorite infused water recipe that catches just the right tastes from the world around you. And enjoy the plethora of vitamins and minerals swimming in the vibrant fruit infused water. Your body and your mind will thank you for it!

Made in the USA
San Bernardino, CA
11 November 2014